Cryptocurrency

How to Invest and Trade with Tips and Tricks to Get the Upper Hand

Jonathan Hardman

Table of Contents

The following eBook is reproduced below with the goal of providing information that is as accurate and reliable as possible. Regardless, purchasing this eBook can be seen as consent to the fact that both the publisher and the author of this book are in no way experts on the topics discussed within and that any recommendations or suggestions that are made herein are for entertainment purposes only. Professionals should be consulted as needed prior to undertaking any of the action endorsed herein.

This declaration is deemed fair and valid by both the American Bar Association and the Committee of Publishers Association and is legally binding throughout the United States.

Furthermore, the transmission, duplication or reproduction of any of the following work including specific information will be considered an illegal act irrespective of if it is done electronically or in print. This extends to creating a secondary or tertiary copy of the work or a recorded copy and is only allowed with express written consent from the Publisher. All additional rights reserved.

The information in the following pages is broadly considered to be a truthful and accurate account of facts and as such any inattention, use or misuse of the information in question by the reader will render any resulting actions solely under their purview. There are no scenarios in which the publisher or the original author of this work can be in any fashion deemed liable for any hardship or damages that may befall them after undertaking information described herein.

Additionally, the information in the following pages is intended only for informational purposes and should thus be thought of as universal. As befitting its nature, it is presented without assurance regarding its prolonged validity or interim quality. Trademarks that are mentioned are done without written consent and can in no way be considered an endorsement from the trademark holder.

Introduction

Congratulations on downloading this book and thank you for doing so.

The following chapters will discuss all the tips that you need to get started with investing in cryptocurrencies. While many people join the cryptocurrency market to send and receive payments, it is also possible to join these networks to invest and make money. In this guidebook, we will take a look at some of the ways that you can invest in digital currencies and make money today.

This guidebook will spend time talking about all the things you can do to invest in digital currencies. We will discuss some of the basics that come with digital currencies, such as how they got started and the benefits of using them. We will also discuss what the blockchain is, how to keep your coins safe from hackers, and some great tips for beginners on how to invest. We will then delve into how to invest in Bitcoin, Ethereum, and some of the other digital currencies that are available.

Many people join a network like Bitcoin to make purchases and keep their identity safe. But when you are ready to join one of these networks as an investment choice to make a lot of money, then make sure to read through this guidebook to help you get started.

There are plenty of books on this subject on the market, thanks again for choosing this one! Every effort was made to ensure it is full of as much useful information as possible. Please enjoy!

Chapter 1: The Beginnings of Cryptocurrency

Cryptocurrencies are starting to take over the world. What started out as a basic idea that no one thought would take off is now one of biggest things throughout the world. Some people join the market to use it as a payment method that is safe and secure. Others join just to check it out. And still others like the idea that they can invest in these digital currencies and make a lot of money in the process.

There are currently more than 1000 cryptocurrencies available on the market, but for the most part, people are concentrating on the top four. These top four include Bitcoin, Ethereum, Ripple, and Litecoin. The first digital currency available on the market was Bitcoin. Bitcoin was released in 2009, along with the blockchain technology that helps run it and keeps it secure. Since that time, the world of digital currencies has grown so much, with people all over the world using and investing in them.

But with all of the hype around these digital currencies, you may be wondering what these currencies are used for?

Cryptocurrencies are used as a form of currency, similar to what you use with the USD and the Euro. These currencies are used digitally, and you are not able to print them off and take them to a local store. However, you can use them to make purchases at various retailers and websites as long as they accept the cryptocurrency you want to use. The market for digital currencies is growing, and there are now more ways than ever to use your coins. For example, it is possible to use cryptocurrencies to donate to a charity, purchase a car from Tesla, buy and sell artwork, buy tickets to games, book hotel rooms, and even crowdfund.

While there are a lot of ways that you can spend your coins, there are also a lot of people who decide to enter these markets as an investment. There are many reasons that you would want to invest in these cryptocurrencies. One reason is that since they have now been around for a little bit, the volatility of cryptocurrencies is starting to calm down. This makes them a little more secure to invest in.

Since these digital currencies are so new, there is a lot of room for them to grow. They can also serve as a hedge against an economic collapse or inflation, and even better choice to go with than using gold. And as more people throughout the world go digital, it is more likely than ever that digital currencies will continue to grow and become the norm as time and technology evolve.

Of course, there are a few things that you will need to watch out for when it comes to using digital currencies. For example, while you do have a good chance to earn a decent profit with digital currencies, it is also easy to lose a lot of money. The digital currency market is still really volatile, and without a lot of history behind these currencies, it is sometimes hard to know when a downturn will happen. If you are someone who doesn't handle much risk in their trades, then these currencies are not the right ones for you.

Another issue that some people have with digital currencies is that they don't necessarily have an inherent value, making them almost worthless. But then, the same thing could be said about fiat currency. While fiat currency used to be backed up by gold, it no longer has this backing and could be seen as just as worthless as digital currencies.

And finally, you must be aware of hacking when you work with these currencies. The whole system is online, and you are not able to print off the money and take it with you. There also isn't any government regulation on the currency, so no one is there to back your money if someone takes it or there is a big downturn in the market. This is a big risk that some people are not willing to take, but it hasn't seemed like a big problem at this time.

While there are a lot of disadvantages that come with digital currencies, and most of them are being worked out as these currencies grow and are around longer, there are a ton of advantages to using these currencies. There is a lot of fluctuation in digital currencies, and for the most part, this fluctuation is going up. For example, it is possible for you to purchase a coin for $30, it could easily go up to $60 and higher within a few days and you get to keep the profits. As long as you watch the market and pick out a good digital currency to work with, you will see your profits rise by huge amounts.

The main reason that so many people like these currencies are that they allow you to remain anonymous online. With all the issues of identity theft and more online, it is a relief to find out that you can still make purchases and send and receive money without people figuring out who you are. With the help of a private address and the blockchain technology, you can join the network without worrying about others finding how who you are.

How are digital currencies different from fiat currencies?

One question that you may have is how digital currencies and fiat currencies are different? If you have heard about Bitcoin, or even used it in the past, you may feel that these currencies are similar and that there really aren't any differences that you can see. However, there are a few differences that you should note before you join in this investment.

First, when it comes to digital currencies, you will not be able to print off paper copies of the coins and carry them around for you.

All of your transactions need to occur online, or through an app on your smartphone. You will purchase the coins online, you will make purchases and send money online, and everything needs to be done online. The only thing that you will ever be able to print off with digital currencies is the private key, and this is only done if you want to store your coin information in cold storage.

This can seem a little bit strange if you are just starting out with digital currencies. But for those who mainly plan to use the currency online, it can seem like regular online shopping. You do need to go through and make the exchange from your fiat currency over to the digital currency before making the purchases, but otherwise, they are similar.

The biggest difference between fiat currency and digital currency is who controls each one. When it comes to your fiat currency, it is going to be controlled by either a government agency or by a big financial institution. They will be able to determine how much currency is printed and how much it is worth. In the case of the United States, the currency isn't even based on the gold standard any longer, so the government has complete control over how the money works.

When it comes to working with digital currencies though, there isn't any type of agency that runs the currency. Instead, they will be based off a complex mathematical equation. There are a certain amount of coins that are designed with the currency, and that is all that is available. Between the mathematical equation and the blockchain, the currency can run on its own and no one can control or mess with the currency. This is a big benefit for a lot of people who choose to use these digital currencies, but it is something new that a lot of people are getting used to.

The differences between fiat currency and digital currency are some of the biggest reasons why so many people are moving online. They like not having a big government agency that controls their money, and they like that they can remain anonymous online when they do their shopping. It may be something that is brand-new, and people are not used to how these work, but digital currencies are here to stay.

Purchasing a digital currency

You will be glad to hear that purchasing these digital currencies is not difficult. But, you do need to have a good idea of what you are looking for. If you want to go with one of the more popular digital currencies, then the best exchange site to work with is Coinbase. Coinbase will allow investors to exchange Litecoin, Ethereum, and Bitcoin. It is likely that digital currencies will be added to this site in the future.

Signing up for Coinbase is pretty easy. You will need to go to the coinbase.com website and then provide a little bit of information. The site will also ask you to use your phone to verify the account. Once all the information is in, you will be able to go to your dashboard and see a lot of information that will help you to do your trades. You can see how much the various coins are currently worth as well as charts about how they have been doing at various intervals over the past year.

When you are ready to get into the market, you need to set up some kind of payment method to make this happen. You can choose between using PayPal, your credit or debit card, or your bank account. Each of these has their own benefits and negatives, and it often depends on what is the easiest for you.

If you would like to have a larger amount of money to invest in initially, then you need to work with your bank account. The bank account option allows you to exchange out more money than the other two options. You do have to deal with a slower transaction time though. When using your bank account, it is often going to take three to five days to get the money transferred over. If you want to get into an investment right now, then the bank account is going to slow you down and may not be the best choice for you.

Using your credit card or PayPal account can be much quicker. These transactions will often be done in a few minutes, making it easier for you to get into the market if there is a sudden shift. If you are doing something like day trading, for example, then working with one of these two options is the best for you. You may not be able to invest as much money at one time with these, but they do allow you to get into the market quickly.

Once you have your chosen payment method in place, you will be able to choose how much money you would like to exchange, and the site will take care of the rest of you. Coinbase will place the money in a wallet that they provide, but you can choose to move the coins over to your wallet when you are all done.

Now, there are some other exchange sites that you can choose to go with, and many of them will be nice as well. It is important that you take care and do your research about an exchange site before you get started. With so many people interested in digital currencies, it should come as no surprise that there are a lot of scammers out there as well. If you do not do your research, it is possible that you will enter into a fake exchange. And if you do this, you will find that they take your payment without ever providing you with your coins.

A good way to see if an exchange site is legitimate is to check the domain name. If you do not see the "HTTPS" in front of the website, then it is not a good idea to exchange coins through it. The HTTPS means that the website is secure and encrypted so if this is not present, it is likely the website is a scam.

Cryptocurrencies are changing the way that money is viewed in our modern world. Instead of being limited by the county we live in, we can now interact and exchange money, make a purchase and do so much more no matter where we are located throughout the world. As more people start to learn about digital currencies and use them for their own needs, it is likely that we will see even more changes come about in our future.

The benefits of cryptocurrency

When it comes to digital currencies, there are a ton of benefits that you are sure to enjoy. These currencies are easy to use, don't have any government regulators controlling them, and anyone can join knowing that their privacy is safe and secure, to name a few. Some of the reasons that so many people like digital currencies and are joining up include:

- Easy to use: Digital currencies are surprisingly easy to use. You don't need to provide a lot of information upfront, you can use the network whenever you would like, and you can live anywhere throughout the world. It is easy to see why so many people are falling in love with digital currencies.

- Safe and secure: Using these digital currencies is safe and secure. Thanks to the blockchain technology, you will be able to send and receive money without anyone being able to see what you are up to online.

- Fast transactions: When you do a transaction through your bank, it can take up quite a bit of time. You have to wait for your bank to process the transaction and then the bank you are sending the money to has to do the same thing. This can result in transactions taking three to five days in most cases. In a world where we are used to things happening right away, this can be really frustrating. With the help of blockchain technology, most digital currencies can complete transactions in a matter of minutes, rather than days.

- Keep your privacy: When you decide to use a digital currency, there are plenty of ways for you to keep your identity a secret. Sometimes you will have to provide a little bit of information to use the exchange site (this varies based on the country you live in), but you can choose a unique address that has no connection back to your own name. In a world where it seems like hackers can steal all your personal information anytime you get online, it is nice to know you can still complete transactions and keep things private at the same time.

- No government regulation: Digital currencies do not have any government controlling them. Instead, they rely on a mathematical equation to help them to run properly and to keep everything fair. For many people, this is a nice change. They are tired of their government being able to control and manipulate their money, and they like working online where no one can find them.

- Anyone can join: As long as you have a connection to the internet and some money to exchange, you will be able to join any of the digital currency networks that you would like. There aren't regulations on where you live or anything else. Compared to trying to open even a simple checking account at a bank, this can be a nice change.

- Low transaction fees: If you have ever tried to make a purchase or send money to someone in another country, you know how expensive the transaction fees can be. This is not something that you need to worry about when it comes to digital currencies. Thanks to the blockchain technology, you can send and receive money anywhere in the world, without having any big fees to work with.

There are many great benefits that you will be able to receive when it comes to working with digital currencies. Whether you are new to the market, you are interested in investing, or you have been around for some time you are sure to enjoy all of these great benefits when you get into digital currencies.

Chapter 2: Blockchain Technology – What Makes Cryptocurrency Work

One issue that some people have with using Bitcoin and some of the other digital currencies is that they are worried about how secure and transparent the system is. There isn't a big government agency or another entity that is in charge of controlling the networks online. This is part of the appeal to many people, but it also raises the issue about how users are supposed to trust the network before they decide to use it. If everything is online, who is to say the transactions will stay private, that someone isn't able to come on and mess with things, or that it is really that safe to use?

This is why the blockchain technology was released at the same time as Bitcoin and this same technology is found in many of the digital currencies that are used. A blockchain is a great tool that not only helps to keep track of the transactions that are going on with digital currencies but helps to provide both the transparency and the security that users are looking for.

The blockchain is basically an online ledger that is able to hold onto any information of value. When it comes to digital currencies, it is going to hold onto information about all the transactions that occur on the network. Anyone who joins the network will be able to look at the blockchain and see the transactions that occur on the network. Anyone will be able to see if there is something that looks off on the network and can prevent people from fudging the numbers or doing something else that is not allowed.

In addition, the blockchain technology helps to keep things safe and secure. Once you are done filling up a chain with all the transactions that you do on the network, your chain will be given a unique code, thanks to the miners, and then it joins the permanent blockchain for the network. You can always look back through your own transactions, but the code the miners give to your particular chain will keep your information safe from others.

So, how do you get one of these chains? As soon as you sign up for a new currency, you will be sent one of these chains. Then, you will slowly work on filling it up with all the transactions that you complete on the network. Some people can fill it up quickly if they do a lot of transactions on the network, and others take some time if they are not as active.

Once the chain is filled up, it will be sent to the permanent blockchain through the network, and you will be sent a new chain to work on. You can continue with this process the whole time you are on the network, and there is no extra work required for you.

Any time that you want to take a look back at your transactions whenever you would like. Think of each of the chains as being your monthly bank statements, and when they connect together, they are your full bank record. You can take a look back at them to check on some of your transactions any time that you have a question about what is going on in the network.

The blockchain technology helps to keep the network safe and secure. Without this kind of technology in place, it is unlikely that these digital currencies would be as successful as they currently are.

What do the miners do?

When it comes to the blockchain technology, miners are very important. These miners are in charge of keeping the whole system safe and ensuring that a hacker is not able to come on and steal information or mess around with the transactions that are on the blockchain. In return, the miners will earn a profit; the amount of that profit will depend on which currency is being used and the current value of that currency.

After you have finished filling up one of your chains for the blockchain, it is going to be sent over to a miner. It is the job of the miner to add a unique code to that chain, effectively hiding all the information that is inside. None of the information about your transactions will be changed, and you will still be able to go through and look at that information anytime you would like, but to others, the information will be changed.

There are a few rules in place to help ensure the codes are secure and that no one will be able to mess with them later on. This also makes it a bit harder for the miners to do their jobs, effectively ensuring that not everyone goes through and does the work within a few days and takes all the available coins.

The first rule is that the code needs to be a unique set of letters and numbers. This sequence cannot be the same as what has been used in other parts of the blockchain. In addition, all the characters need to be connected so that if you change one part of the code, it will change up all the other parts as well. This makes it easier to spot if someone got onto the ledger and tried to make changes without authorization. It only takes the changing of on character to mess up the whole blockchain. There are also some regulations about how many zeroes need to be present at the beginning of each code before the system accepts it.

As you can see, creating one of these codes can be a bit of a challenge, and it does take time. You will need to have specialized computers and specs on that computer to keep up with the work at hand. In addition, you must compete against other miners who are trying to do the same thing as you to win the reward. You could easily work on several codes and never earn a profit because of all the competition.

The work of the miners will help to benefit the currency network. You will help to slowly release more coins into the market, helping it keep up with demand without issues of inflation. Plus, there is the benefit of providing security and privacy for all the users on the network. Since there isn't a government agency or other entity controlling the digital currency network, the miners are basically the ones responsible for this.

The good news is that the miners will be rewarded as well. Each currency will provide a reward to a miner who can successfully complete one of the codes. The amount that you will earn varies based on which digital currency you work with, but it can be a nice profit if you can do it successfully. In the case of Bitcoin, for example, you can earn 25 coins each time you complete one of these codes.

Other ways blockchain can be used

While the main application for blockchain right now is for Bitcoin and other digital currencies, there are so many other ways that the blockchain technology can be utilized. Many businesses and companies are starting to realize the value of this technology and have started to create their own applications to better serve customers in ways that were not possible in the past.

For example, in Europe, several major banks have come together to create a blockchain. These may be rival banks in different countries, but they recognize how using a combined blockchain can help them to better serve their customers. Instead of making their customers pay higher fees and wait several days to send money back and forth, they can work with the blockchain that these banks provide to get the transactions done for a lower cost and within a few minutes. This can help to facilitate trade between countries and has helped bring in quite a few customers for these banks.

The financial world is not the only thing who could benefit from the blockchain technology. Many other industries are already looking to develop their own blockchain technology. Insurance companies can use it to help speed up claims, countries can use it for voting, and even hotels and driving services could use it as a way to make reservations without as many issues. The possibilities for blockchain are almost endless, making it the perfect choice for bringing us into the modern world.

The blockchain technology may have been released at the same time as Bitcoin, but it is a technology all on its own. Many other industries can develop this kind of technology to help make their businesses more effective. As long as the business needs to add items of value to a ledger, the blockchain ledger can help to make this happen.

Chapter 3: Keeping Your Currencies Safe

One thing that you need to consider when you start investing in digital currencies is how to keep the coins as safe as possible. There is quite a bit of money to be made with these currencies, and because of this, there are a lot of hackers who are interested in taking your coins from you. Since no one is around to monitor your accounts or to set up regulations to protect you like you can get from a bank, you can be out of luck if you do not protect your information and keep your coins in a safe and secure place.

Luckily, there are a few steps that you can take that will help you to keep your currencies away from the hackers and as safe as possible. Making sure you pick out the right wallet to store the coins in and learning how to keep your personal information anonymous can make all the difference when it comes to how protected your coins will stay. Let's take a look at some of the different ways that you can protect your coins, so the money stays with you, and not with a hacker.

Pick out a good wallet

One of the best things that you can do to keep your coins safe is to pick out a safe and secure wallet. Since you are working with digital currencies, you will not be able to get the coins and carry them around with you. These coins will always remain digital and need to be stored in a wallet, either online, on your computer, or in cold storage, until you are ready to use them.

The first option that you can go with is an online wallet. If you use an exchange site to get your coins, your coins will be deposited into an online wallet through that site. Many beginners will leave their coins in this online wallet because they are easier to access when you want to use the coins. However, the online wallet is the most likely to be hacked. So far, these online wallets have proven relatively safe. Many hackers are trying to get onto the databases of these online wallets. If they are successful, they would have access to all the coins from all the users on that wallet.

If you plan to use the coins you have right away, and they won't be stored in the wallet for long, then using an online wallet is just fine. For those who are looking to store their coins for some time while investing, it is much safer to go with one of the other wallet types.

For those who are looking to invest in these digital currencies, it is best to go with a wallet that is a little more secure. The first option is a hardware wallet. This wallet allows you to take the coins offline and store them on your computer. There are a few programs to help you with this and you simply download the wallet folder onto your computer. Then, when you are ready to move the coins over, you can easily do so.

This method can be much better when you are planning on investing. The hacker will need to get access to your computer before they can take the coins. It is a good idea to update your antivirus and other protections on your computer before doing this though to ensure that no one can get your information. This method will take a few extra steps to use the coins, but as an investor, you will not use the coins that often.

If you plan to go with a long-term investment, then you need to consider cold storage. Cold storage takes the coins off the computer completely. You will simply print off the private key that controls your coins and then store the key in a safe place. Do not leave this key out in the open or someone could still get ahold of the key and take your coins. Many consider putting it in a safety security box to keep it out of the way.

With this method, it is going to take a bit more work when you want to use the coins. You will need to re-enter the information into the computer before being able to use the coins. And you will need to update the private key that you print off each time that you add or take coins out of your account. But when it comes to security, this is one of the best options you can go with.

If you would really like to keep your information safe, you can consider working with a few wallets. That way, if someone does take your coins or mess with your account, you have a few backups that will help you to prove yourself and get the coins all back. Always remember that when you change your coins, either adding them or taking them out, you need to update all of your wallets. It is not going to do you much good if you have the wrong or outdated information in one of your wallets.

Picking a good wallet is critical to the security of your coins. There are too many hackers out there who would love nothing more than to get ahold of your coins and use them for their own. You need to be proactive to ensure that you are always in control of your own coins and that no one else will take your money.

Learn how to stay anonymous

One of the best things that you can do to protect your coins is made sure that your personal information stays hidden. While the blockchain technology is safe and secure, it is still possible for anyone to see the transactions that happen on this ledger. If a hacker sees a lot of transactions that have your first and last name on them, it is much easier for them to trace that information right back to your wallet.

When you sign up for an account with one of these currency networks, you can pick out the address that you want to use. It is best if you can come up with something unique. Some sites will even provide you with a unique address of random letters and numbers if you are having trouble coming up with one on your own. The more random the address is, the easier it is for you to keep your information safe and secure.

If you plan to do a lot of transactions on the network, it may be wise to consider changing up the address on a regular basis. The creators of Bitcoin actually suggested that users change out their address after each transaction they completed to maintain their privacy. Most people do not want to change their address this often, but doing it on occasion can make it harder for hackers to trace things back to you.

It is so important that you learn how to keep your coins as safe as possible. Many hackers would love to swoop in and take away your coins, and there isn't much that you can do if this happens. Taking the right precautions, like the ones above, can help you to keep your coins with you all the time.

Chapter 4: Investing in Bitcoin

When you are looking to invest in a digital currency, it is likely that the first one you will consider is Bitcoin. Bitcoin has seen some huge increases in value over the last year. Despite having a short downturn at the end of 2017, it is steadily rising and is still one of the best digital currencies to work with. Many people around the world have heard about Bitcoin and are currently using it, and there are a lot of options when it comes to investing in this currency.

You will get to choose from a variety of investing methods when it comes to Bitcoin. Some people choose to invest in the blockchain technology, some will go with a long-term strategy like the buy and hold strategy, and even stock market trading and day trading can be relatively successful when using this digital currency. Let's take a look at some of the different methods that you can use to get started investing in Bitcoin.

Invest in a Bitcoin company

There are several Bitcoin companies available in the stock market, similar to what you find with some of the other big businesses throughout the world. This means that even if you do not want to purchase the coins directly, you are still able to invest in the Bitcoin network and see some results.

For this, you need to treat the investment similar to what you would with any other business on the stock exchange. You should do some research on the various charts and figures that are available on Bitcoin, perform a fundamental analysis, and come up with a good strategy that will get you started. While Bitcoin is doing really well right now and seems like a great investment, it is always important to remember there is some risk involved so take the proper steps to keep your money safe.

Invest in the blockchain

Some people get into Bitcoin because they are really interested in the blockchain technology that helps run Bitcoin. They see a lot of potentials that come with this technology, and they want to get in on the ground floor and make some money in the process. There are a few different ways that you can invest in the blockchain depending on how much money and technical knowledge you have.

If you have a bit of technical background, you can consider developing your own blockchain to use, or even an app that can be used with a current Bitcoin blockchain. There are a lot of users of Bitcoin right now and being able to create one of these for users can definitely bring in some money.

For those who do not have any technical knowledge, you can choose to invest in a developer or company who is creating new blockchain technology. This is more commonly seen in Ethereum since that platform offers a free blockchain to get started, but there are some opportunities to use as well.

Start your own business

Many people will choose to accept Bitcoin as a form of payment. This helps to open up the market they can work in because there are a lot of people who want to pay with Bitcoin, but not a lot of companies who will accept this payment. If you already own a business or are thinking about starting a new business, then consider accepting Bitcoin to pay for your services or products.

Accepting Bitcoin is pretty easy. You simply need to sign up for your own unique Bitcoin address and for a wallet. Then add a link to your website that will allow the customer to choose Bitcoin as a payment method when they get that far. If the customer clicks on that link, you will need to send them your Bitcoin address. The customer can send you the payment, and then you send over the product or service. It is that simple.

Use the buy and hold strategy

The buy and hold strategy is one of the most common investment strategies that new investors will work on. It is simple, and as long as you watch the market and make sure no big downturns occur, you will be able to make a lot of money without a lot of work.

The idea behind the buy and hold strategy is that you will purchase the number of coins that you will like and then store them in a secure wallet. Then, outside of watching the market to see if there are any indicators of a reversal, you will just leave your coins alone in the market. Since Bitcoin is steadily increasing in value, you should see that your coins are worth more within a few months, just by leaving them in the market.

For example, back in February of 2017, the value of Bitcoin reached about $2500. Then by December of 2017, the value of Bitcoin had skyrocketed to over $18,000 a coin. If you had held onto your coins for a few months and then exchanged them out at this time, you could have made more than $15,000 in profit for each coin that you owned.

This requires very little work compared to some of the other trading methods. You should watch the market and read the news to find out if the market does go down. This way, you can get out and protect your investment before the value goes down too much and you lose money.

Day trading

Another option that you can go with to invest in Bitcoin is day trading. While the main market of Bitcoin sees a steady increase in the value of the coins, if you look at the charts each day, you will see that the value has a lot of ups and downs. These show how people come into and leave the market from day to day. As a day trader, you need to use these little ups and downs to your advantage.

To really be a day trader, you must make a purchase of coins at some time during the day and then you will sell them, hopefully for a profit, during the same day. This takes a lot of time researching and watching the market, and you often only will make a little money on each trade. But over time, these little profits can add up to a lot of money for the successful trader.

With day trading, you need to learn what the market average for the coins is. When you can figure this out, you will watch the market to find out when the coins are below market average and make a purchase. This allows you to get the coins for a nice discount. Then, once the coins go back to market value or go above that market value, you can sell the coins and make a profit. The amount will not be a ton, but if you do this many times throughout the week, it can add up.

This is a great method to make money in the digital currency market, but you do need to have the time and dedication to keep up with it. In addition, when figuring out the costs of doing this investment, remember that each time you exchange out your currency, you will be charged a small fee by your exchange site. This is usually not a large amount, but when you exchange on a regular basis, it can add up.

Chapter 5: Investing in Ethereum

While Bitcoin is still seen as one of the biggest digital currencies on the market right now, Ethereum is a name that is starting to grow quite a bit as well. Ethereum is a bit different than Bitcoin, but it has gained its own special place in the digital currency market, and it can be highly profitable. While Bitcoin concentrates on being a payment method, similar to what you would find with PayPal or a credit card, Ethereum is more of a platform that helps promote the growth of the blockchain technology.

The coins that are used on Ethereum, known as Ether, are not used as a regular payment method. You will not find a ton of stores online that will accept these coins and they are not really used to help with purchases. Instead, the Ether is used to help support developers who are working on new applications of the blockchain technology. An investor can purchase some of these Ether, send them over as a payment to a developer, and this helps the developer to get more work done.

Let's back up a little bit and look more at how Ethereum works. The Ethereum platform is all about supporting the growth of blockchain technology. As we discussed earlier in this guidebook, the blockchain is not only critical to helping these digital currencies to grow. The blockchain technology can be used in many other industries including banking, insurance, contracts and so much more. There are so many industries that can benefit from this kind of technology and many are willing to pay for others to develop these new platforms for them.

The biggest problem with the further development of blockchain is that it is really complicated to create. The blockchain is really complicated, which is part of the appeal of how it works, and it takes some time to start from the very beginning. With only a few developers available who had the time and knowledge to create one of these platforms from the beginning, it is no wonder that the spread of this technology has been so slow.

With the help of Ethereum, things have already changed, and it is likely we will see even more changes in the future. Ethereum provides an open-sourced blockchain that anyone is able to use. This means that you can go on the Ethereum network and use the blockchain that is available on there. You can make changes, add to it, take things away, and so much more to create your own program with this technology.

There is so much that developers can do with this open-sourced blockchain. Some will work for a company and create a platform that the company can use to conduct business. Some developers may have an idea of a new platform that could benefit a few different businesses, and they decide to create it and then sell that platform when they are done. And some may simply have a new application or an addition to an existing platform that they want to design and then sell to the users of the original platform. Since they don't need to start from the very beginning, they can get the work done fairly quickly, saving time and money.

There are a lot of possibilities when it comes to using this open-sourced blockchain, and many developers are jumping on board to see what they can create. And there are certainly a lot of different companies who are willing to pay for their own blockchain to make it easier to work with customers.

So, how can you benefit as an investor from this platform? The market for blockchain is hot right now, but some developers need an investor to provide them with money while they work on a project. You can take a look at some of the different blockchain options that are available on the platform and then choose which one you would like to invest in.

Once you make your decision, you can then provide the developers with some Ether (the two parties will be able to agree on the price that works the best for them). Once the blockchain platform or application is done, the developer will pay you the investment back, along with the interest or the other agreed upon terms, and you will make money from the work that you did.

How do you ensure that you will get paid when you invest through Ethereum? Since this is a digital currency, there will not be a third party around to enforce anything on the network. However, you will fill out a smart contract with the other party, and this will hold the two of you to the agreement.

A smart contract is basically a self-executing contract. You and the other party will be able to use these contracts to set out the agreement you want to work with. When both sides have held up their end of the bargain, the terms will be executed. So, if the developer agreed to pay you a certain amount when the platform is done, or at another agreed upon date, the contract would make sure this happens.

This is one of the main ways that people choose to invest in the blockchain technology. Those who are developing the platform will be able to get the money that is needed to finish their work, and you can earn a profit when they are done and sell the platform. You can also choose to develop a platform through the Ethereum network, you can help to sell some of these platforms, and so much more.

Ethereum may be a newer digital currency than Bitcoin and some of the others, and it works differently than what you will find with other digital currencies. But it is a great way to help expand out the blockchain technology and is a great investment opportunity for those who want to get into the market but feel that other currencies are not right for them.

Chapter 6: Investing in Other Digital Currencies

While Bitcoin and Ethereum are considered some of the biggest digital currencies that you can invest in right now, there are a lot of other choices that you can go with. Choosing one of these other digital currencies can make a big difference in how much you can make. For example, Bitcoin has been around for some time and has a really high value right now. But going with another option, like one of the options below, can make it easier to get into the market because the current value is much lower.

Each currency is going to be a little bit different. Some are currencies like Bitcoin and can be invested in the same way. Others are more platforms or can help to facilitate trading within the other digital currencies. Learning how to invest in each of these currencies will make it easier to determine if the currency is the right investment for you. Let's take a look at some of the other major digital currencies that you can invest in and how to get started with them.

Bitcoin Cash

Over the past few years, there have been a number of complaints about Bitcoin. The original Bitcoin was developed with only 21 million coins available. These coins would slowly be added to the market as miners completed their codes to keep the chains of the blockchain secure. Many people worry that this amount of coins will not be enough, especially when considering how many people throughout the world are starting to use these digital currencies. There are also some issues with the speed of Bitcoin.

Bitcoin Cash is meant to be an alternative to Bitcoin and is meant to help solve some of the problems that we talked about before. It is easy to get started with Bitcoin Cash. You can either start out right away with the Bitcoin Cash. Or, if you already have Bitcoin, you are allowed to switch these out for Bitcoin Cash and start using these if you would like.

From here, you can often choose to work with the same investment types as you did with Bitcoin. Right now there are not as many businesses that are accepting Bitcoin Cash as they are with Bitcoin and it is taking some competition away from other digital currencies. However, it is starting to grow, especially because it is much faster than using Bitcoin with all the same benefits, and you will see the value grow in no time.

Investing in Litecoin

You can also choose to invest in Litecoin. In fact, this is one of the options that are available through the popular exchange site known as Coinbase. Litecoin is a peer to peer currency that will enable you to send instant, low-cost payments, to anyone you would like to throughout the world. It is completely decentralized and opens sourced, making it similar to Bitcoin in these ways. It is one of the top digital currencies, following Ethereum and Bitcoin and often tied with Ripple.

So, how is Litecoin different from Bitcoin and some of the other digital currencies. First, Litecoin is going to work with a software algorithm to mine units. This can help prevent individuals from making customer computers to mine the currency. In addition, the transaction times with Litecoin are one of the fastest of all the currencies. Right now, Litecoin can get transactions done in less than three minutes, while it usually takes Bitcoin about ten minutes.

In addition, Litecoin is one of the cheapest of the three big currencies, which makes it a good choice for investors. As of June 2017, you would need to spend over $3000 to start with Bitcoin and Ethereum was more than $300. However, Litecoin was trading at $40, so it was much easier to get started with.

Litecoin is a currency just like Bitcoin, so you will be able to use many of the same investment options to make this work. You can exchange your fiat currency over to Litecoin through Coinbase and then use day trading, invest in a company, or even the buy and hold strategy to make money. With the lower cost of entry and the rising popularity of Litecoin, this is a good option to get into before the value goes way up.

Investing in Dash

Some people choose to work with a currency known as Dash. This is a cryptocurrency that has made it its mission to solve some of the problems that have come up with Bitcoin. It is known as an open-source cryptocurrency that split off from Litecoin in 2014. This currency is mainly working on solving the issue of speed that is found in Bitcoin. With Bitcoin, it can take minutes to resolve a transaction, something that isn't going to work in a world where things need to be done instantly.

The biggest problem is that purchasing Dash is not going to be the easiest, which can slow down how fast it becomes popular. To purchase the coins, you will first need to go to Coinbase and purchase some Bitcoin. You can then use your Bitcoin to go to Bitsane and purchase the Dash that you want to use. Until that issue is solved, it may be hard for Dash to take off. There are rumors that Coinbase may be adding in Dash to their network, but that has not happened yet.

Once you have your Dash coins, you will be able to invest in it like you do other currencies. The buy and hold strategy may work the best for this one because it allows you some flexibility to keep your coins while waiting for more people to hear about it. With Bitcoin slowing down all the time because more and more people are getting onto the network, and the fact that the popular Coinbase may add Dash to its dashboard, it is likely that the value of Dash is going to continue growing in the near future.

Investing in Dogecoin

Dogecoin is a digital currency that is similar to Bitcoin. It was introduced in December of 2013. This currency has made it through bearish and bullish markets and is often seen as a tipping currency. What this means is that you can tip someone with Dogecoin rather than using upvotes and likes on social media.

Right now, Dogecoin is not worth all that much, but this can make it a good one to invest in because the price will be so low to join. How this market works is that when you are on a certain website or a social media page, you can tip the other person for the hard work that they do. It is not going to provide them with a lot of money, but as a tip, and if a lot of people tip at the same time, the owner could make some money.

Since Dogecoin is sometimes known as a joke currency right now, it is a bit hard to make it grow, and it is still not huge compared to some of the others. However, in the past year, Dogecoin has seen a big increase, and it is predicted that it will keep on growing. Since you can get many coins for less than a dollar, this could be a good investment to start with. If Dogecoin continues in the same path for the next few years, you could spend just a few dollars to get started and then make a big profit in the future.

Another option that you can go with is to start your own website or social media site and provide entertaining material to your viewers. You can then add a button that allows people to pay you in Dogecoin if they would like to tip or use your page. It may not be much, but if the page becomes popular and does well, you can earn some money with these coins. Hold the coins in your wallet for a little bit, and you may be able to earn more as the currency increases in value.

Investing in Ripple

Another popular digital currency that you can work with is known as Ripple. Ripple is known as a settlement network that is used to transfer any currency to someone no matter where they are located in the world. Rather than having to use systems like the Western Union or SWIFT and waiting for days to get the money to the right place (and dealing with high fees in the process), you can get the transaction done within a few seconds.

Right now, Ripple focuses its attention on working with banks. This works well because Ripple offers a cost-effective and efficient way for customers to send payments all around the world.

Think about how expensive it can be to send money throughout the world. Each step that you have to take to send the money is going to add to the fees, making it really expensive. But with the help of Ripple, you can send this money to someone else (as long as both of you have a Ripple wallet), and the fees will stay low.

Users can send money to each other as well. You would simply exchange out your fiat currency for Ripple and then send it to someone else who has a Ripple wallet. The other user will be able to change it back to whichever fiat currency they would like to use. It doesn't matter where you send the money, it is only going to cost a few cents for each transaction, making it more effective than other methods. You also won't have to worry about which currency each person is using because Ripple can handle all of them.

With all of the different exchanges that go on throughout the world, it makes sense that investing in Ripple is going to grow in no time. People all around the world want to trade and send money to each other. And since Ripple can handle any type of currency that you send through it, there are fewer restrictions on who can use it. You can use either your fiat currency or even other digital currencies, and send them to people across the world.

There are many different types of digital currencies that you can choose to invest in. Some will provide you with a good return on investment, and others are not going to make it past a few weeks in the market. There is a lot of competition with these digital currencies, and you need to be able to pick which ones are likely to stick around and do the best. Picking a good one can help you to earn a lot of money in the process when it starts to increase in value. However, picking out a bad currency can lead you to lose all of your investment in a few weeks. Learning how to manage your currencies and how to pick out the right ones can make a big difference in how well you will do in the digital currency market.

Chapter 7: Tips and Tricks to Help Make Investing in Cryptocurrencies Easier

Working in digital currencies can be a great way for you to make a profit. These currencies are growing like crazy, and you are sure to make a profit as long as you enter the market at the right time, and you know how to read the market. However, investing in digital currencies can still carry some risks with it. Learning how to reduce your risks as much as possible can make it so much easier for you to earn a profit, without having to worry about potential losses as much. Let's take a look at some of the ways that you can reduce your risks and earn a great income with digital currencies.

Ask for help

As a beginner, there is no way that you can know everything about investing in digital currencies. Some things may confuse you, and you may have some questions along the way. Asking for help from someone who knows what they are doing, rather than trying to figure it all out on your own, can be the best way for you to learn how to invest properly.

There are several people you can work with when it comes to asking for help. It is likely that you got into cryptocurrency investing because someone you know talked about how much they made. If this is true, it may be a good idea to ask them for advice when you are stuck. Some beginners even consider hiring a broker to help them make their trades and to ask advice from as they move through the market.

Pick out one strategy

Picking out a good strategy to work with will make all the difference when it comes to trading in digital currencies. There are many strategies that you can use, and the one you work with will often depend on your chosen cryptocurrency as well as with whether you wish to invest short-term or long-term. All of the strategies have the potential to make you money as long as you use them properly.

The biggest issue with many strategies is that the investor either doesn't know how to use them or the investor switches between a few strategies during the same trade. Most strategies cannot be used at the same time, or mixed together, during the same trade and still produce results. It is fine to switch out of strategies from one trade to another. But when you are inside a trade, you need to finish the same trade that you started with. This can be hard sometimes, but if you switch out strategies in the middle of a trade, there is a high probability that you will end up failing.

Keep the emotions away from the investment

Keeping your emotions out of your investment is so important if you want to actually earn money. Emotions get in the way and make it almost impossible to make sound decisions on any of your investments. If you are not careful, you will keep on the market too long and either lose more money or lose all the profit you have earned so far.

Having a solid trading plan is so important to helping you avoid the emotions. This trading plan is meant to outline all the steps that you need to take to see a profit with a chosen currency. In it, you should outline when you plan to enter the market, when you plan to exit the market, the strategy you would like to use, and how much you are comfortable with losing before getting out of the market.

Even the most level-headed person in the world can become emotional when they start to see their money going away in digital currencies. They are more likely to stay in the market too long if they see that they are in a losing position. They may hope that the market will turn around and if they just hold on a little longer, they can regain the money. Or they may be greedy, and when they see that they are earning profits, they will keep in the market and hope that they will keep seeing more profits the longer they stay in.

This rarely works. When you start losing money in the market, the trend is likely to continue. And if you stay in the market for too long, even your profits can start to fade. It is much better to come up with a good trading plan that outlines all that you need to do. Stick with this, and you will see more consistent profits over time, and fewer losses.

Understand the currency you are working with

This guidebook spent some time talking about the various digital currencies that you can work with. However, there are so much more that we didn't get a chance to discuss. There are more than 1000 digital currencies, and they all will work in different ways. Some will work on a new payment method like Bitcoin while others will be more of a platform for the blockchain like Ethereum. And still, others work in a different manner altogether.

Since all of these currencies work in different ways, it is important that you fully understand the way that your currency works before you join in. Jumping into a digital currency simply because it has a lot of hype around it can be disastrous for your investment. You need to actually know something about the currency and how it works. The more you know about your currency, the easier it is to understand how the currency makes you money and you can then determine the best times to enter and leave the market.

Diversify your portfolio

Many investors who choose to get into the market of cryptocurrencies will pick out one currency to work with and then never look at anything else. This strategy may be fine if you are short on capital to get started with. But when it comes to growing your investment and still reducing your risk, it is best if you can diversify your portfolio as much as possible.

Diversifying your portfolio means that you will put your money into at least two different investment types. The more investments that you can do at once, the less risk you are taking on. It is possible for one of your digital currencies to take a big hit. If all your money is in that one digital currency, you stand to deal with some big loses. But if you spread out your capital between three or more digital currencies, you can split up the risk, and you won't lose as much.

In the beginning, when your capital is low, it is fine to invest in just one or two digital currencies. As you start to earn more profits though, it is best if you decide to invest in more options to reduce your risks. In addition, you can consider investing in other investment choices, like the stock market, real estate, or something else, to help you to expand out your portfolio even more. The more places you can invest your money, the less risk you will deal with.

Have an exit strategy

No matter what strategy you choose to go with, you should make sure that you have an exit strategy right from the beginning. This can help you to keep your emotions out of the game from the beginning and will make it easier for you to stick with your plan rather than losing money. And you must make sure that once you set the exit strategy, you stick with it no matter what.

First, you must make sure to set up an exit strategy for protecting your losses. Think about how much you are willing to lose on the trade if things end up going poorly and not working out well for you. This is where you need to set your first stop point. If the market does go downhill and it starts to lose value, you will exit the market no matter what. You may lose a little bit of money, but it is much less than you will lose if you stay in the market any longer.

Without this kind of exit strategy, it is too easy to consider staying in the market. You may see that your money is starting to fade away, and you will want to stay in the market in the hopes of the market turning around. You can become desperate and hope that things will get better, but this rarely happens. It is much better to cut your losses and get yourself out of the market at the right time. You can always get back in the market later, but if you stay in the market too long and lose all your money, it becomes almost impossible to get in later on.

You should also consider putting an exit strategy in place for the number of profits that you earn. This may seem like a crazy thing to do, but it can help you to get out of the market and keep your profits around, rather than staying into the market and getting caught in a quick downturn that takes all the profits away. Ahead of time, decide how much profit you are happy with making. Once the market gets there, you need to leave and enjoy the profits. If the market continues to go up, you can always get back in later on.

Once you have set these exit points, you must stick with them. It does not matter how the market behaves or how much you hope that the market will keep going up, or that it will reverse. You must stick with these exit points to reduce your risks as much as possible.

Working in digital currencies is an exciting market right now. There are a lot of people who have made their fortunes by joining the right digital currency market at the right time. The tips above will help you as a beginner to get into the market and to see results in no time while reducing your risks at the same time.

Conclusion

Thank you for making it through to the end of this book, let's hope it was informative and able to provide you with all of the tools you need to achieve your goals whatever they may be.

The next step is to decide which cryptocurrency you would like to invest in. We talked about some of the biggest names in cryptocurrencies. You can choose to work with these options or use some of the tips and tricks we discussed to invest in one of the other digital currencies that are on the market. These currencies have a lot of potentials and will continue to grow in the future, and it makes sense to put your money there and watch it grow.

Each digital currency is different, which will provide you with a lot of choices for investing your money. And right now, no other investment opportunity is going to provide you with a good return on investment as Bitcoin, Ethereum and some of the other digital currencies.

Finally, if you found this book useful in any way, a review on Amazon is always appreciated!

www.ingramcontent.com/pod-product-compliance
Lightning Source LLC
Chambersburg PA
CBHW071156220526
45468CB00003B/1055